DIABE GASTROPARESIS DIET COOKBOOK

The Complete Delicious Low Sugar Recipes for Gastric Pain Relief

AMY J. CLEAVES

TABLE OF CONTENTS

INTRODUCTION

Living with diabetes is a challenge all on its own, demanding constant vigilance, balance, and lifestyle changes to maintain blood sugar stability and overall health.

Add gastroparesis to the mix, and the journey becomes even more complex. For those who experience the daily struggles of diabetes alongside gastroparesis, food can feel less like nourishment and more like a hurdle.

The symptoms of gastroparesis—ranging from nausea and bloating to delayed stomach emptying—can significantly complicate blood sugar management, making meal planning an overwhelming task.

The purpose of this book is to make that task easier and more achievable. This Diabetes Gastroparesis Diet Cookbook is designed to help you craft meals that will not only meet the nutritional needs of someone managing diabetes but will also be gentle on a stomach affected by gastroparesis.

This combination of low-fat, low-fiber, and easily digestible foods, combined with strategies for meal timing and portion control, is intended to help you enjoy food again.

By understanding how diet affects both conditions and by making meal choices that support stable blood sugar levels and ease gastroparesis symptoms, you'll be better equipped to navigate your dietary needs with confidence.

Managing diabetes with gastroparesis demands a unique approach, one that takes into account both blood sugar management and digestive comfort. There are countless resources for people with diabetes, and some for those with gastroparesis, but very few are designed to address both together.

This cookbook serves as a tailored resource to help you navigate a dual diagnosis with a practical, positive approach.

Understanding Diabetes

Diabetes is a chronic condition that affects millions of people worldwide. It occurs when the body either doesn't produce enough insulin or doesn't use insulin effectively, leading to elevated blood sugar levels.

These high blood sugar levels, if left unchecked, can damage various organs and systems in the body. There are several types of diabetes, each with unique characteristics and implications for management. However, for all types, maintaining stable blood sugar is a central goal.

The two main types of diabetes are Type 1 and Type 2, but there is also gestational diabetes and a range of other variations, such as prediabetes. Understanding these different types can help clarify why dietary management is essential.

- **Type 1 Diabetes:** This is an autoimmune condition where the body attacks insulin-producing cells in the pancreas. People with Type 1 diabetes must take insulin daily, and their blood sugar levels can be highly sensitive to dietary changes, exercise, and other factors.

- **Type 2 Diabetes:** In Type 2 diabetes, the body either resists the effects of insulin or doesn't produce enough insulin to maintain normal glucose levels. It is often managed with a combination of lifestyle changes, medications, and sometimes insulin. Type 2 is the most common form of diabetes and is heavily influenced by diet and physical activity.

- **Gestational Diabetes:** This form occurs during pregnancy and can increase the risk of both the mother and child developing diabetes later in life. Managing blood sugar levels is crucial to prevent complications during pregnancy.

While each type of diabetes has different management strategies, dietary management is a universal factor for all. Understanding the foods that support blood sugar stability is crucial, especially for those who must balance it with the dietary restrictions required for gastroparesis.

For individuals with diabetes, maintaining stable blood glucose levels is critical for preventing both immediate complications (such as hypoglycemia or hyperglycemia) and long-term health risks, including cardiovascular disease, kidney damage, and neuropathy.

Proper management often involves monitoring carbohydrate intake, being mindful of food portion sizes, and adjusting the timing of meals.

When gastroparesis is added to the mix, however, controlling blood sugar becomes much more challenging. Gastroparesis slows the digestion of food, which can cause erratic blood sugar levels.

Food that stays too long in the stomach may lead to delayed absorption of carbohydrates, causing unexpected spikes or drops in blood glucose. To effectively manage both conditions, people with diabetes and gastroparesis need to pay careful attention to both what they eat and when they eat it.

The digestive tract, like many other body systems, is impacted by diabetes. High blood sugar levels over time can damage nerves, including the vagus nerve, which controls the movement of food through the digestive system.

Damage to this nerve is often the cause of gastroparesis in people with diabetes, leading to symptoms such as nausea, bloating, and a feeling of fullness after only a few bites.

For individuals with diabetes, gastroparesis can make it difficult to manage blood sugar levels effectively. Large, high-fiber, or high-fat meals can worsen symptoms and delay the absorption of carbohydrates, causing unpredictable blood sugar spikes or drops. This is why a diet that focuses on small, frequent, low-fat, low-fiber meals is essential.

By understanding these dynamics, we can begin to approach diet not just as a way to fuel the body, but as a tool for symptom management and blood sugar stability. This book will provide dietary guidelines and recipes specifically designed to achieve these goals, helping you navigate a path to better health and wellness.

Understanding Gastroparesis

Gastroparesis is a condition that slows or stops the movement of food from the stomach to the small intestine, even when there is no physical blockage.

It's often described as "stomach paralysis," and while it affects people for various reasons, it's commonly linked to nerve damage—specifically, the vagus nerve, which controls the muscles in the stomach.

When the vagus nerve is damaged, often as a complication of diabetes, it disrupts the body's natural digestive rhythm, leaving food lingering in the stomach for much longer than it should.

In a healthy digestive system, food moves steadily from the stomach to the intestines, where it can be digested further and absorbed into the bloodstream. This steady movement is crucial for nutrient absorption and blood sugar management.

But in people with gastroparesis, the stomach muscles don't function properly, and food isn't broken down or pushed into the intestines as efficiently. This delayed emptying can cause bloating, nausea, and even vomiting, making eating feel uncomfortable and challenging.

People with diabetes are particularly susceptible to gastroparesis because prolonged high blood sugar levels can damage the vagus nerve. The condition is most commonly seen in people with Type 1 diabetes, but it can also affect those with Type 2.

For people with both diabetes and gastroparesis, maintaining stable blood sugar levels becomes even harder due to the unpredictability of food absorption.

Gastroparesis can present a range of symptoms that vary in severity and can impact daily life significantly:
- **Nausea and Vomiting:** Food sitting in the stomach for too long can trigger nausea and lead to vomiting undigested food.

- **Bloating and Discomfort:** Delayed stomach emptying often causes bloating, a sensation of fullness after only a few bites, and discomfort in the upper abdomen.

- **Appetite Loss:** With bloating and nausea as constant symptoms, appetite often diminishes, leading to weight loss and nutritional deficiencies.

- **Erratic Blood Sugar Levels:** For people with diabetes, delayed stomach emptying means carbohydrates are absorbed at an unpredictable rate, causing sudden blood sugar spikes or delayed lows, which can be difficult to manage.

These symptoms can be frustrating and challenging, especially when combined with the demands of diabetes management. The discomfort can make regular eating difficult, but frequent, small meals with low fiber and low fat are generally recommended to keep symptoms manageable.

If you suspect you have gastroparesis, talk to your healthcare provider, as they may suggest tests like a gastric emptying study to evaluate how quickly food moves through your stomach.

While there's currently no cure for gastroparesis, there are treatment options available to manage symptoms:

- **Medications:** There are medications that help stimulate stomach muscle contractions, aiding food movement. Others may help alleviate symptoms like nausea.

- **Dietary Modifications:** A specialized diet is one of the most effective ways to manage gastroparesis, which is why this cookbook is focused on guiding you through meal planning.

- **Lifestyle Changes:** Some people benefit from eating smaller meals, sitting upright after meals, and including gentle physical activity like walking to encourage digestion.

Understanding these basics will help you manage gastroparesis symptoms and make informed dietary choices.

Managing Diabetes Gastroparesis with Diet

When living with both diabetes and gastroparesis, diet becomes your most powerful tool. The right foods and eating habits can provide the nourishment you need while reducing symptoms and maintaining blood sugar stability.

Because gastroparesis slows down stomach emptying, the focus of the diet is on easily digestible foods that don't linger in the stomach. Fiber, fat, and large meal sizes tend to exacerbate symptoms, so the dietary strategy typically involves low-fiber, low-fat options and smaller, more frequent meals.

For diabetes, this approach aligns well, as smaller, steady doses of carbohydrates prevent sudden spikes in blood sugar.

The core principles of a diabetes gastroparesis diet include:

- **Low-Fiber Foods:** Fiber is beneficial for most people, but it's difficult to digest and can slow stomach emptying. Opt for foods that are low in fiber, such as peeled fruits and cooked vegetables, while avoiding high-fiber choices like raw leafy greens and whole grains.

- **Low-Fat Options:** High-fat foods also slow digestion and can worsen symptoms of gastroparesis. Choose low-fat proteins, avoid fried or fatty foods, and incorporate cooking methods like steaming and baking.

- **Small, Frequent Meals:** Eating smaller portions more frequently helps manage both blood sugar and digestion. Aim to eat every 2-3 hours, with each meal containing moderate portions of easily digestible foods.

- **Hydration:** Staying hydrated is essential for health and can also help prevent gastroparesis symptoms. Drinking fluids with meals should be avoided, however, as they can take up stomach space and worsen bloating. Instead, sip water between meals.

Now that we understand the core principles, let's look at specific food groups and how to approach them:

- **Proteins:** Lean protein sources are ideal, as they're low in fat and easy on the stomach. Consider foods like skinless poultry, white fish, eggs, and tofu. These sources are gentle on digestion and provide essential nutrients.

- **Carbohydrates:** Focus on simple, low-fiber carbohydrates that digest quickly. White bread, white rice, and peeled or canned fruits (in their natural juice) are good options. Avoid whole grains and high-fiber foods like beans and lentils.

- **Fruits and Vegetables:** Opt for well-cooked or canned versions of low-fiber vegetables, such as carrots and squash, and fruits like bananas, peaches, and applesauce. Avoid raw vegetables and high-fiber fruits like oranges or berries.

- **Dairy:** If dairy is tolerated, choose low-fat options like yogurt or lactose-free milk. Some people with gastroparesis find dairy challenging, so experiment with different options if you have trouble.

- **Fats and Oils:** Use fats sparingly. Choose small amounts of healthy oils like olive oil when necessary, but avoid heavy sauces, butter, and fatty meats.

The way you eat can be just as important as what you eat when managing gastroparesis. Here are a few strategies to make eating more comfortable and symptom-free:

- **Eat Slowly:** Take time to chew each bite thoroughly. Eating slowly allows the stomach to process each bit of food, making it easier on digestion.
- **Stay Upright After Meals:** Sitting upright after eating encourages gravity to assist digestion, helping food pass through the stomach more smoothly.
- **Avoid Lying Down After Eating:** It's best to wait at least 2-3 hours before lying down after meals to prevent symptoms from worsening.
- **Choose Pureed or Soft Foods When Possible:** Pureed foods can be easier to digest and may reduce symptoms. Smooth soups, mashed vegetables, and soft grains are all good options.

Managing diabetes gastroparesis with diet is all about making food choices that are gentle on the stomach while supporting blood sugar stability.

Breakfast Recipes

Creamy Banana Oatmeal

 2 servings   15 minutes

INGREDIENTS

- 1 cup quick-cooking oats
- 2 cups water
- 1 ripe banana, mashed
- 1/2 teaspoon cinnamon
- 1 tablespoon honey (optional)
- 1/4 cup skim milk or lactose-free milk

DIRECTIONS

1. In a saucepan, bring the water to a boil.
2. Stir in the oats and reduce the heat to low. Cook for 1-2 minutes, stirring occasionally, until the oats are soft.
3. Add the mashed banana and cinnamon. Mix well and cook for an additional minute.
4. Remove from heat and stir in the milk for creaminess. Sweeten with honey if desired.
5. Serve warm.

Nutritional Info per Serving: Calories: 180 | Carbs: 34g | Protein: 5g | Fat: 2g

Scrambled Eggs with Spinach

 2 servings   🕐 10 minutes

INGREDIENTS

- 4 large eggs (or 2 whole eggs + 4 egg whites for lower cholesterol)
- 1 cup fresh spinach, chopped (use well-cooked if sensitive)
- 1 tablespoon low-fat milk or lactose-free milk
- Salt and pepper to taste
- Cooking spray or 1 teaspoon olive oil

DIRECTIONS

1. In a bowl, whisk together the eggs, milk, salt, and pepper until well blended.
2. Heat a non-stick skillet over medium heat and lightly coat with cooking spray or oil.
3. Add the chopped spinach and sauté for about 1-2 minutes until wilted.
4. Pour the egg mixture into the skillet and gently stir, cooking until the eggs are just set, about 3-4 minutes.
5. Remove from heat and serve immediately.

Nutritional Info per Serving: Calories: 150 | Carbs: 1g | Protein: 13g | Fat: 10g

Yogurt Parfait with Soft Fruits

 2 servings   🕐 5 minutes

INGREDIENTS

- 2 cups plain low-fat yogurt (or lactose-free yogurt)
- 1 cup soft fruits (such as ripe bananas or canned peaches in light syrup, drained)
- 2 tablespoons honey (optional)
- 1/4 teaspoon vanilla extract (optional)

DIRECTIONS

1. In a bowl, mix the yogurt with vanilla extract if using.
2. In serving glasses or bowls, layer half of the yogurt, followed by half of the soft fruits.
3. Repeat the layers with the remaining yogurt and fruits.
4. Drizzle honey on top if desired.
5. Serve chilled.

Nutritional Info per Serving: Calories: 130 | Carbs: 20g | Protein: 7g | Fat: 2g

Apple Cinnamon Smoothie

 2 servings   5 minutes

INGREDIENTS

- 1 medium ripe apple, peeled and cored
- 1 cup low-fat yogurt or lactose-free yogurt
- 1/2 cup unsweetened applesauce
- 1/2 teaspoon ground cinnamon
- 1/2 cup water or low-fat milk (adjust for desired consistency)

DIRECTIONS

1. In a blender, combine the peeled apple, yogurt, applesauce, cinnamon, and water or milk.
2. Blend on high until smooth and creamy. If the mixture is too thick, add more water or milk to reach your desired consistency.
3. Pour into glasses and serve immediately.

Nutritional Info per Serving: Calories: 150 | Carbs: 30g | Protein: 6g | Fat: 2g

Soft Scrambled Tofu

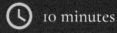

🍴 2 servings 🕐 10 minutes

INGREDIENTS

- 1 cup soft tofu, crumbled
- 1 tablespoon low-sodium soy sauce
- 1 tablespoon low-fat milk or lactose-free milk
- 1/4 teaspoon turmeric (for color, optional)
- Cooking spray or 1 teaspoon olive oil

DIRECTIONS

1. In a bowl, combine the crumbled tofu, soy sauce, milk, and turmeric. Mix well.
2. Heat a non-stick skillet over medium heat and lightly coat with cooking spray or oil.
3. Pour the tofu mixture into the skillet and gently stir. Cook for about 4-5 minutes until heated through and slightly firm but still soft.
4. Serve warm.

Nutritional Info per Serving: Calories: 100 | Carbs: 3g | Protein: 10g | Fat: 5g

Mashed Avocado Toast on Soft Bread

 2 servings   🕐 10 minutes

INGREDIENTS

- 1 ripe avocado
- 2 slices of soft, white bread (or gluten-free bread)
- 1 tablespoon lemon juice
- Salt to taste

DIRECTIONS

1. Toast the bread lightly until just warm (optional, for preference).
2. In a bowl, mash the avocado with a fork. Stir in the lemon juice and salt.
3. Spread the mashed avocado evenly on the slices of bread.
4. Serve immediately as an open-faced toast.

Nutritional Info per Serving: Calories: 180 | Carbs: 20g | Protein: 4g | Fat: 10g

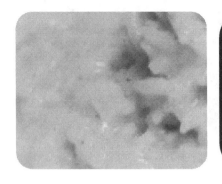

Rice Porridge with Almond Milk

 2 servings   🕐 20 minutes

INGREDIENTS

- 1/2 cup white rice
- 2 cups unsweetened almond milk (or other low-fat milk of choice)
- 1 tablespoon honey (optional)
- 1/2 teaspoon vanilla extract (optional)

DIRECTIONS

1. Rinse the rice under cold water and drain.
2. In a saucepan, combine the rice and almond milk. Bring to a boil, then reduce the heat to low and simmer, stirring occasionally, for about 15-20 minutes, until the rice is soft and creamy.
3. Add honey and vanilla extract if desired, and stir to combine.
4. Serve warm.

Nutritional Info per Serving: Calories: 150 | Carbs: 28g | Protein: 2g | Fat: 3g

Cottage Cheese and Peach Bowl

 2 servings   5 minutes

INGREDIENTS

- 1 cup low-fat cottage cheese
- 1/2 cup canned peaches (in light syrup or water, drained)
- 1 teaspoon cinnamon
- 1 tablespoon honey (optional)

DIRECTIONS

1. Divide the cottage cheese between two bowls.
2. Top each bowl with half of the peaches.
3. Sprinkle with cinnamon and drizzle honey on top if desired.
4. Serve chilled or at room temperature.

Nutritional Info per Serving: Calories: 120 | Carbs: 16g | Protein: 10g | Fat: 2g

Soft Boiled Eggs with White Toast

 2 servings 10 minutes

INGREDIENTS

- 4 large eggs
- 2 slices white bread (or gluten-free bread if needed)
- Salt and pepper to taste

DIRECTIONS

1. In a small saucepan, bring water to a boil. Carefully lower the eggs into the boiling water.
2. Reduce the heat to medium and let the eggs cook for 6 minutes for soft-boiled or 8 minutes for slightly firmer yolks.
3. While the eggs cook, toast the bread lightly if desired.
4. Peel the eggs and serve with the toast. Season with salt and pepper to taste.

Nutritional Info per Serving: Calories: 150 | Carbs: 15g | Protein: 11g | Fat: 6g

Smooth Ricotta Pancakes

 2 servings 15 minutes

INGREDIENTS

- 1/2 cup low-fat ricotta cheese
- 1/4 cup all-purpose flour
- 1 large egg
- 1 tablespoon honey (optional)
- 1/4 teaspoon vanilla extract
- Cooking spray or 1 teaspoon olive oil

DIRECTIONS

1. In a bowl, whisk together the ricotta, flour, egg, honey, and vanilla until smooth.
2. Lightly coat a non-stick skillet with cooking spray or oil and heat over medium-low heat.
3. Pour small spoonfuls of batter onto the skillet to make mini pancakes. Cook each side for 2-3 minutes or until golden.
4. Serve warm.

Nutritional Info per Serving: Calories: 180 | Carbs: 18g | Protein: 9g | Fat: 6g

Pumpkin Spice Cream of Rice

🍴 2 servings   🕐 10 minutes

INGREDIENTS

- 1/2 cup cream of rice cereal
- 1 1/2 cups water or almond milk
- 1/4 cup canned pumpkin puree (unsweetened)
- 1/2 teaspoon pumpkin spice or cinnamon
- 1 tablespoon honey (optional)

DIRECTIONS

1. In a small pot, bring the water or almond milk to a boil.
2. Stir in the cream of rice, reduce heat to low, and cook for 3-5 minutes, stirring constantly until thickened.
3. Add the pumpkin puree and pumpkin spice, stirring to combine. Cook for another 1-2 minutes until warmed through.
4. Sweeten with honey if desired and serve warm.

Nutritional Info per Serving: Calories: 160 | Carbs: 32g | Protein: 2g | Fat: 2g

Baked Apples with Greek Yogurt

 2 servings   🕐 15 minutes

INGREDIENTS

- 2 medium apples, peeled and cored
- 1/2 teaspoon cinnamon
- 1 tablespoon honey (optional)
- 1/2 cup low-fat Greek yogurt (or lactose-free yogurt)

DIRECTIONS

1. Preheat the oven to 350°F (175°C).
2. Place the apples in a baking dish and sprinkle with cinnamon. Drizzle honey on top if desired.
3. Bake the apples for 10-12 minutes, until soft and warm.
4. Serve each apple with a spoonful of Greek yogurt.

Nutritional Info per Serving: Calories: 130 | Carbs: 25g | Protein: 4g | Fat: 2g

Vanilla Rice Pudding

 2 servings   20 minutes

INGREDIENTS

- 1/2 cup cooked white rice
- 1 cup almond milk (unsweetened)
- 1/2 teaspoon vanilla extract
- 1 tablespoon honey (optional)
- Pinch of cinnamon (optional)

DIRECTIONS

1. In a small saucepan, combine the cooked rice and almond milk over medium heat.
2. Add vanilla extract and stir occasionally, cooking until the mixture thickens, about 10-12 minutes.
3. Sweeten with honey and add cinnamon if desired. Stir to blend flavors.
4. Serve warm or chilled.

Nutritional Info per Serving: Calories: 120 | Carbs: 24g | Protein: 2g | Fat: 2g

Soft Poached Eggs with Mashed Potatoes

 2 servings 15 minutes

INGREDIENTS

- 2 large eggs
- 1 medium potato, peeled and diced
- 1/4 cup low-fat milk or lactose-free milk
- Salt and pepper to taste

DIRECTIONS

1. In a small pot, boil the diced potato until soft, about 8-10 minutes. Drain and mash with milk, salt, and pepper.
2. While the potato cooks, bring a small pot of water to a simmer.
3. Carefully crack each egg into the water and poach for 3-4 minutes until whites are set but yolks are soft.
4. Serve each egg over a small portion of mashed potato.

Nutritional Info per Serving: Calories: 140 | Carbs: 15g | Protein: 8g | Fat: 5g

Warm Applesauce with Cottage Cheese

 2 servings   5 minutes

INGREDIENTS

- 1 cup unsweetened applesauce
- 1/2 cup low-fat cottage cheese
- 1/2 teaspoon cinnamon
- 1 tablespoon honey (optional)

DIRECTIONS

1. In a small saucepan, gently warm the applesauce over low heat for 2-3 minutes.
2. Pour the warm applesauce into bowls and top with cottage cheese.
3. Sprinkle with cinnamon and drizzle honey if desired.
4. Serve immediately.

Nutritional Info per Serving: Calories: 120 | Carbs: 18g | Protein: 6g | Fat: 2g

Lunch Recipes

Creamy Chicken and Rice Soup

 2 servings   🕐 30 minutes

INGREDIENTS

- 1/2 cup cooked white rice
- 1/2 cup cooked shredded chicken breast (skinless)
- 2 cups low-sodium chicken broth
- 1/4 cup low-fat milk or lactose-free milk
- Salt and pepper to taste
- Fresh herbs like parsley (optional, finely chopped)

DIRECTIONS

1. In a saucepan, combine the chicken broth, shredded chicken, and cooked rice. Bring to a gentle simmer over medium heat.
2. Add the milk and stir until the soup is warm and slightly creamy.
3. Season with salt and pepper to taste, and garnish with parsley if desired.
4. Serve warm.

Nutritional Info per Serving: Calories: 180 | Carbs: 20g | Protein: 15g | Fat: 4g

Soft Baked Cod with Mashed Potatoes

 2 servings 🕐 25 minutes

INGREDIENTS

- 2 small cod fillets (or any soft, white fish)
- 1 tablespoon lemon juice
- Salt and pepper to taste
- 1 medium potato, peeled and cubed
- 1/4 cup low-fat milk or lactose-free milk
- 1/2 teaspoon olive oil

DIRECTIONS

1. Preheat the oven to 375°F (190°C). Place the cod fillets on a baking sheet lined with parchment paper. Drizzle with lemon juice and season with a pinch of salt and pepper.
2. Bake the fish for 15-18 minutes or until the fish flakes easily with a fork.
3. While the fish bakes, boil the potato cubes until soft, about 10 minutes. Drain and mash with milk and a small amount of olive oil.
4. Serve the baked cod alongside the mashed potatoes.

Nutritional Info per Serving: Calories: 210 | Carbs: 22g | Protein: 20g | Fat: 3g

Egg Drop Soup with Soft Tofu

🍴 2 servings 🕐 15 minutes

INGREDIENTS

- 2 cups low-sodium chicken or vegetable broth
- 1/2 cup soft tofu, cubed
- 1 large egg, beaten
- 1/2 teaspoon sesame oil (optional, for flavor)
- Salt and pepper to taste
- Chopped chives for garnish (optional)

DIRECTIONS

1. In a saucepan, bring the broth to a gentle simmer over medium heat. Add the tofu cubes.
2. Slowly pour the beaten egg into the broth in a thin stream, stirring gently to create egg ribbons.
3. Season with salt, pepper, and sesame oil, if using.
4. Garnish with chopped chives and serve warm.

Nutritional Info per Serving: Calories: 100 | Carbs: 2g | Protein: 7g | Fat: 6g

Lemon-Herb Chicken with Creamy Polenta

 2 servings 🕐 30 minutes

INGREDIENTS

- 1 small chicken breast, skinless and boneless
- 1 tablespoon lemon juice
- 1/4 teaspoon dried thyme or rosemary
- Salt and pepper to taste
- 1/2 cup quick-cooking polenta
- 1 1/2 cups water
- 1/4 cup low-fat milk or lactose-free milk

DIRECTIONS

1. Preheat the oven to 375°F (190°C). Place the chicken breast in a small baking dish, drizzle with lemon juice, sprinkle with thyme, and season with salt and pepper.
2. Cover the dish with foil and bake for 20-25 minutes or until the chicken is cooked through.
3. While the chicken bakes, bring the water to a boil in a saucepan. Stir in the polenta and reduce heat to low, cooking for 5 minutes while stirring continuously.
4. Add the milk to the polenta for a creamy texture, then serve alongside the baked chicken.

Nutritional Info per Serving: Calories: 220 | Carbs: 24g | Protein: 18g | Fat: 4g

Tuna and Avocado Rice Bowl

 2 servings   🕐 10 minutes

INGREDIENTS

- 1 can (5 oz) tuna in water, drained
- 1/2 small ripe avocado, diced
- 1 cup cooked white rice, warm
- 1 teaspoon lemon juice
- Salt and pepper to taste

DIRECTIONS

1. In a bowl, mix the tuna with lemon juice, salt, and pepper.

2. In serving bowls, divide the warm rice, then top with the tuna and diced avocado.

3. Serve immediately, stirring gently to combine before eating.

Nutritional Info per Serving: Calories: 220 | Carbs: 24g | Protein: 18g | Fat: 6g

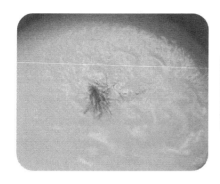

Carrot and Ginger Soup

2 servings | 20 minutes

INGREDIENTS

- 2 medium carrots, peeled and diced
- 1/2 teaspoon fresh ginger, grated
- 2 cups low-sodium vegetable broth
- 1/4 cup low-fat milk or lactose-free milk
- Salt and pepper to taste

DIRECTIONS

1. In a medium pot, combine the diced carrots, ginger, and vegetable broth. Bring to a boil, then reduce heat and simmer for about 15 minutes, until the carrots are soft.
2. Use an immersion blender or regular blender to puree the soup until smooth.
3. Stir in the milk, then season with salt and pepper to taste. Serve warm.

Nutritional Info per Serving: Calories: 110 | Carbs: 20g | Protein: 3g | Fat: 2g

Simple Shrimp and Rice Bowl

 2 servings   🕐 15 minutes

INGREDIENTS

- 1/2 cup cooked white rice
- 6-8 small shrimp, peeled and deveined
- 1 teaspoon lemon juice
- Salt and pepper to taste
- 1/4 teaspoon dried basil or parsley (optional)

DIRECTIONS

1. Heat a small, non-stick skillet over medium heat. Add shrimp and cook for about 2-3 minutes per side, until pink and opaque.
2. Season with lemon juice, salt, pepper, and basil or parsley if desired.
3. Place the cooked rice in bowls and top with shrimp. Serve warm.

Nutritional Info per Serving: Calories: 180 | Carbs: 20g | Protein: 15g | Fat: 3g

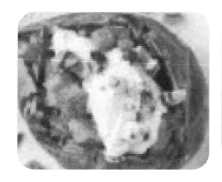

Baked Sweet Potato with Yogurt and Cinnamon

 2 servings 20 minutes

INGREDIENTS

- 1 medium sweet potato
- 1/2 cup low-fat Greek yogurt or lactose-free yogurt
- 1/4 teaspoon ground cinnamon
- 1 teaspoon honey (optional)

DIRECTIONS

1. Preheat the oven to 400°F (200°C). Pierce the sweet potato with a fork and bake for about 15-20 minutes or until tender.
2. Slice the sweet potato open and top each half with a spoonful of yogurt.
3. Sprinkle with cinnamon and drizzle honey if desired. Serve warm.

Nutritional Info per Serving: Calories: 140 | Carbs: 26g | Protein: 4g | Fat: 1g

Broiled Tilapia with Mashed Carrots

 2 servings   20 minutes

INGREDIENTS

- 2 small tilapia fillets
- 1 teaspoon lemon juice
- Salt and pepper to taste
- 2 medium carrots, peeled and chopped
- 1/4 cup low-fat milk or lactose-free milk

DIRECTIONS

1. Preheat the broiler on low. Place tilapia fillets on a baking sheet lined with foil, season with lemon juice, salt, and pepper.
2. Broil for about 5-6 minutes, or until the fish flakes easily with a fork.
3. Meanwhile, steam or boil the carrots until soft, about 10-12 minutes. Drain and mash with milk until smooth.
4. Serve the tilapia alongside the mashed carrots.

Nutritional Info per Serving: Calories: 160 | Carbs: 15g | Protein: 18g | Fat: 2g

Turkey and Zucchini Bowl

 2 servings   🕐 20 minutes

INGREDIENTS

- 1/2 cup ground turkey (lean, skinless)
- 1 small zucchini, peeled and finely chopped
- 1/2 cup cooked white rice
- 1/4 teaspoon dried basil
- Salt and pepper to taste
- 1 teaspoon olive oil

DIRECTIONS

1. In a skillet, heat olive oil over medium heat. Add ground turkey and cook until browned, breaking it up into small pieces as it cooks.
2. Add the chopped zucchini and cook for an additional 5-7 minutes, until the zucchini is tender and the turkey is fully cooked.
3. Stir in the basil, and season with salt and pepper to taste.
4. Serve over a bowl of warm cooked rice.

Nutritional Info per Serving: Calories: 220 | Carbs: 18g | Protein: 20g | Fat: 6g

Baked Sole with Creamy Mashed Cauliflower

 2 servings   🕐 25 minutes

INGREDIENTS

- 2 sole fillets (or any other mild, white fish)
- 1 tablespoon lemon juice
- Salt and pepper to taste
- 1/2 head cauliflower, cut into florets
- 1/4 cup low-fat milk or lactose-free milk

DIRECTIONS

1. Preheat the oven to 375°F (190°C). Place the sole fillets on a baking sheet lined with parchment paper. Drizzle with lemon juice and season with salt and pepper.
2. Bake the fish for 12-15 minutes or until it flakes easily with a fork.
3. Meanwhile, steam the cauliflower florets until soft, about 10-12 minutes. Drain and mash with milk until creamy.
4. Serve the baked fish alongside the mashed cauliflower.

Nutritional Info per Serving: Calories: 180 | Carbs: 10g | Protein: 20g | Fat: 4g

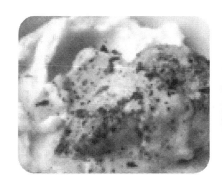

Chicken and Potato Puree

 2 servings 20 minutes

INGREDIENTS

- 1 small chicken breast, skinless and boneless
- 1 medium potato, peeled and diced
- 1/4 cup low-fat milk or lactose-free milk
- Salt and pepper to taste
- 1/4 teaspoon dried parsley (optional)

DIRECTIONS

1. Boil the chicken breast in water until fully cooked, about 10-12 minutes. Remove and shred into small pieces.
2. In another pot, boil the diced potato until tender, about 8-10 minutes. Drain and mash with milk until smooth.
3. Mix the shredded chicken into the mashed potatoes, adding salt, pepper, and parsley if desired.
4. Serve warm.

Nutritional Info per Serving: Calories: 190 | Carbs: 15g | Protein: 18g | Fat: 3g

Soft Turkey and Rice Meatballs

 2 servings   🕐 25 minutes

INGREDIENTS

- 1/2 cup lean ground turkey
- 1/4 cup cooked white rice
- 1 tablespoon low-fat milk
- Salt and pepper to taste
- 1/4 teaspoon dried oregano (optional)

DIRECTIONS

1. In a mixing bowl, combine the ground turkey, cooked rice, milk, salt, pepper, and oregano. Mix well and shape into small meatballs.
2. In a non-stick skillet, add a small amount of water or broth to prevent sticking, then cook the meatballs over medium heat for about 10-12 minutes, turning occasionally, until they are cooked through.
3. Serve with an extra spoonful of cooked rice or mashed potatoes, if desired.

Nutritional Info per Serving: Calories: 180 | Carbs: 15g | Protein: 18g | Fat: 5g

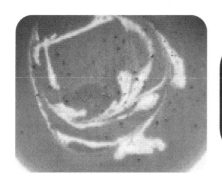

Mild Pumpkin Soup

 2 servings   🕐 15 minutes

INGREDIENTS

- 1 cup canned pumpkin puree (unsweetened)
- 1 1/2 cups low-sodium vegetable or chicken broth
- 1/4 cup low-fat milk or lactose-free milk
- Salt and pepper to taste
- 1/4 teaspoon ground ginger (optional)

DIRECTIONS

1. In a saucepan, combine the pumpkin puree and broth. Bring to a simmer over medium heat and stir until smooth.
2. Add the milk, salt, pepper, and ginger, if using, and heat for another 2-3 minutes until warmed through.
3. Serve warm and garnish with a small sprinkle of fresh herbs if desired.

Nutritional Info per Serving: Calories: 80 | Carbs: 12g | Protein: 3g | Fat: 2g

Poached Chicken with Mashed Sweet Potato

 2 servings   25 minutes

INGREDIENTS

- 1 small chicken breast, skinless and boneless
- 1 medium sweet potato, peeled and cubed
- 1/4 cup low-fat milk or lactose-free milk
- Salt and pepper to taste

DIRECTIONS

1. In a small pot, bring water to a boil, add the chicken breast, and poach for 12-15 minutes until fully cooked. Remove and shred into small pieces.
2. In another pot, boil the sweet potato cubes until soft, about 10-12 minutes. Drain and mash with milk until smooth.
3. Serve the shredded chicken over a small portion of mashed sweet potato. Season with a pinch of salt and pepper, if desired.

Nutritional Info per Serving: Calories: 190 | Carbs: 18g | Protein: 20g | Fat: 2g

Dinner Recipes

Baked Cod with Soft Polenta

 2 servings   🕐 25 minutes

INGREDIENTS

- 2 small cod fillets
- 1 teaspoon lemon juice
- Salt and pepper to taste
- 1/2 cup quick-cooking polenta
- 1 1/2 cups water
- 1/4 cup low-fat milk or lactose-free milk

DIRECTIONS

1. Preheat the oven to 375°F (190°C). Place the cod fillets on a baking sheet lined with parchment paper, drizzle with lemon juice, and season with salt and pepper.
2. Bake the fish for 12-15 minutes or until it flakes easily with a fork.
3. Meanwhile, bring water to a boil in a saucepan. Slowly add the polenta, stirring constantly. Lower the heat and cook for 5 minutes, stirring until smooth.
4. Stir in the milk to make the polenta creamy and serve warm with the baked cod.

Nutritional Info per Serving: Calories: 210 | Carbs: 22g | Protein: 19g | Fat: 4g

Steamed Chicken and Carrot Puree

 2 servings 20 minutes

INGREDIENTS

- 1 small chicken breast, skinless and boneless
- 2 medium carrots, peeled and chopped
- 1/4 cup low-fat milk or lactose-free milk
- Salt and pepper to taste

DIRECTIONS

1. Place the chicken breast in a steamer basket over boiling water and steam for 12-15 minutes until fully cooked, then slice or shred into small pieces.
2. In a separate pot, steam or boil the carrots until soft, about 10-12 minutes. Drain and mash the carrots with milk until smooth.
3. Serve the shredded chicken over the carrot puree. Season lightly with salt and pepper, if desired.

Nutritional Info per Serving: Calories: 170 | Carbs: 15g | Protein: 18g | Fat: 3g

Simple Salmon and Potato Mash

 2 servings 🕐 20 minutes

INGREDIENTS

- 1 small salmon fillet
- 1/4 teaspoon dried dill or parsley
- Salt and pepper to taste
- 1 medium potato, peeled and cubed
- 1/4 cup low-fat milk or lactose-free milk

DIRECTIONS

1. Place the salmon in a non-stick pan with a little water and cook over medium heat for about 5-7 minutes on each side, until fully cooked. Season with dill, salt, and pepper.
2. While the salmon cooks, boil the potato cubes until soft, about 10-12 minutes. Drain and mash with milk until smooth.
3. Serve the cooked salmon alongside the potato mash.

Nutritional Info per Serving: Calories: 200 | Carbs: 18g | Protein: 20g | Fat: 6g

Herb-Infused Tilapia with Mashed Cauliflower

 2 servings   20 minutes

INGREDIENTS

- 2 small tilapia fillets
- 1 teaspoon lemon juice
- 1/4 teaspoon dried thyme or parsley
- Salt and pepper to taste
- 1/2 head cauliflower, cut into florets
- 1/4 cup low-fat milk or lactose-free milk

DIRECTIONS

1. Preheat a non-stick skillet over medium heat. Place the tilapia fillets in the skillet, add a splash of water, and cook for 3-4 minutes on each side until flaky and cooked through. Drizzle with lemon juice and sprinkle with thyme, salt, and pepper.
2. In a separate pot, steam the cauliflower florets until tender, about 10 minutes. Drain and mash with milk until creamy.
3. Serve the tilapia fillets alongside the mashed cauliflower.

Nutritional Info per Serving: Calories: 180 | Carbs: 10g | Protein: 20g | Fat: 3g

Soft-Baked Chicken and Rice Casserole

 2 servings   🕐 25 minutes

INGREDIENTS

- 1/2 cup cooked white rice
- 1 small chicken breast, diced
- 1/4 cup low-sodium chicken broth
- 1/4 cup low-fat milk or lactose-free milk
- Salt and pepper to taste
- 1/4 teaspoon dried basil or parsley (optional)

DIRECTIONS

1. Preheat the oven to 375°F (190°C). In a small baking dish, mix the cooked rice, diced chicken, chicken broth, and milk.
2. Season with salt, pepper, and basil or parsley if desired.
3. Cover the dish with foil and bake for 20 minutes or until the chicken is fully cooked and the rice has absorbed the liquid.
4. Let cool slightly before serving.

Nutritional Info per Serving: Calories: 210 | Carbs: 20g | Protein: 18g | Fat: 4g

Soft-Baked Cod with Sweet Potato Puree

 2 servings   20 minutes

INGREDIENTS

- 2 small cod fillets
- 1 teaspoon lemon juice
- Salt and pepper to taste
- 1 medium sweet potato, peeled and cubed
- 1/4 cup low-fat milk or lactose-free milk

DIRECTIONS

1. Preheat the oven to 375°F (190°C). Place the cod fillets in a baking dish, drizzle with lemon juice, and season with salt and pepper.
2. Cover with foil and bake for 12-15 minutes or until the cod is fully cooked and flakes easily with a fork.
3. While the cod bakes, boil or steam the sweet potato cubes until tender, about 10 minutes. Drain and mash with milk until smooth.
4. Serve the baked cod alongside the sweet potato puree.

Nutritional Info per Serving: Calories: 200 | Carbs: 18g | Protein: 20g | Fat: 2g

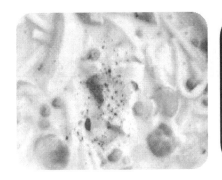

Creamy Chicken and Carrot Soup

 2 servings   🕐 30 minutes

INGREDIENTS

- 1 small skinless chicken breast, diced
- 2 medium carrots, peeled and sliced
- 2 cups low-sodium chicken broth
- 1/4 cup low-fat milk or lactose-free milk
- Salt and pepper to taste

DIRECTIONS

1. In a saucepan, bring the chicken broth to a boil. Add the diced chicken and sliced carrots. Cook for about 15 minutes until the chicken is fully cooked and the carrots are tender.
2. Remove from heat and let cool slightly. Use an immersion blender to puree the soup until smooth. If using a regular blender, allow it to cool before blending.
3. Stir in the milk and season with salt and pepper. Heat gently before serving.

Nutritional Info per Serving: Calories: 160 | Carbs: 12g | Protein: 20g | Fat: 3g

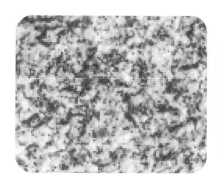

Quinoa and Spinach Frittata

 2 servings　　 25 minutes

INGREDIENTS

- 1/2 cup cooked quinoa
- 2 large eggs
- 1/4 cup low-fat milk or lactose-free milk
- 1/2 cup fresh spinach, chopped
- Salt and pepper to taste
- 1 teaspoon olive oil

DIRECTIONS

1. Preheat the oven to 350°F (175°C). In a mixing bowl, whisk together the eggs, milk, salt, and pepper. Stir in the cooked quinoa and chopped spinach.
2. In a small oven-safe skillet, heat olive oil over medium heat. Pour in the egg mixture and cook for about 3-4 minutes, until the edges start to set.
3. Transfer the skillet to the oven and bake for 10-12 minutes, or until the frittata is fully set and slightly golden on top.
4. Allow to cool slightly before slicing and serving.

Nutritional Info per Serving: Calories: 180 | Carbs: 15g | Protein: 12g | Fat: 8g

Easy Vegetable Risotto

 2 servings 🕐 30 minutes

INGREDIENTS

- 1/2 cup Arborio rice
- 1 cup low-sodium vegetable broth
- 1/2 cup water
- 1/4 cup low-fat milk or lactose-free milk
- 1/2 cup diced zucchini (peeled)
- Salt and pepper to taste
- 1 teaspoon olive oil

DIRECTIONS

1. In a saucepan, heat the olive oil over medium heat. Add the Arborio rice and cook for 1-2 minutes, stirring constantly.
2. Gradually add the vegetable broth and water, one ladle at a time, stirring frequently until the liquid is absorbed before adding more.
3. After about 15 minutes, add the diced zucchini and continue to cook for an additional 5 minutes, or until the rice is creamy and tender.
4. Stir in the milk and season with salt and pepper before serving warm.

Nutritional Info per Serving: Calories: 210 | Carbs: 40g | Protein: 6g | Fat: 4g

Poached Shrimp with Creamy Polenta

 2 servings   🕐 20 minutes

INGREDIENTS

- 1/2 pound raw shrimp, peeled and deveined
- 2 cups water
- 1/2 cup quick-cooking polenta
- 1/4 cup low-fat milk or lactose-free milk
- Salt and pepper to taste
- 1 teaspoon lemon juice

DIRECTIONS

1. In a saucepan, bring 2 cups of water to a boil. Add the shrimp and cook for about 2-3 minutes, or until they turn pink and opaque. Drain and set aside.
2. In a separate pot, bring 2 cups of water to a boil, then gradually whisk in the polenta. Cook for about 5 minutes, stirring constantly until thickened.
3. Stir in the milk, salt, and pepper to the polenta until smooth and creamy.
4. Serve the poached shrimp over the creamy polenta and drizzle with lemon juice.

Nutritional Info per Serving: Calories: 220 | Carbs: 26g | Protein: 18g | Fat: 4g

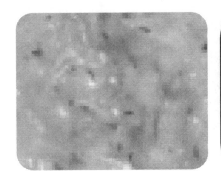

Chicken Broth with Rice and Egg

 2 servings 15 minutes

INGREDIENTS

- 2 cups low-sodium chicken broth
- 1/2 cup cooked white rice
- 2 large eggs
- Salt and pepper to taste
- 1 teaspoon olive oil (optional)

DIRECTIONS

1. In a saucepan, bring the chicken broth to a simmer.
2. Add the cooked rice to the broth and heat for about 2-3 minutes until warmed through.
3. In a separate bowl, beat the eggs. Slowly drizzle the beaten eggs into the hot broth while stirring gently to create egg ribbons.
4. Season with salt and pepper and serve warm.

Nutritional Info per Serving: Calories: 180 | Carbs: 20g | Protein: 12g | Fat: 6g

Soft Baked Eggplant with Cheese

 2 servings   🕐 30 minutes

INGREDIENTS

- 1 small eggplant, sliced into rounds
- 1/2 cup low-fat ricotta cheese
- 1/4 cup low-fat mozzarella cheese, shredded
- 1 teaspoon olive oil
- Salt and pepper to taste

DIRECTIONS

1. Preheat the oven to 375°F (190°C). Place the eggplant slices on a baking sheet lined with parchment paper and brush lightly with olive oil. Season with salt and pepper.
2. Bake the eggplant slices for about 15 minutes or until tender.
3. Remove from the oven and top each slice with a spoonful of ricotta cheese and a sprinkle of mozzarella cheese.
4. Return to the oven and bake for an additional 5-7 minutes, until the cheese is melted and bubbly.

Nutritional Info per Serving: Calories: 200 | Carbs: 12g | Protein: 14g | Fat: 10g

Turkey and Rice Stuffed Peppers

 2 servings   🕐 35 minutes

INGREDIENTS

- 2 small bell peppers (red or yellow), halved and seeds removed
- 1/2 cup cooked ground turkey (lean)
- 1/2 cup cooked white rice
- 1/4 cup low-sodium chicken broth
- Salt and pepper to taste
- 1 teaspoon dried oregano (optional)

DIRECTIONS

1. Preheat the oven to 350°F (175°C). In a mixing bowl, combine the cooked ground turkey, cooked rice, chicken broth, salt, pepper, and oregano (if using).
2. Fill each bell pepper half with the turkey and rice mixture.
3. Place the stuffed peppers in a baking dish and cover with foil. Bake for 25 minutes, or until the peppers are tender.
4. Serve warm.

Nutritional Info per Serving: Calories: 220 | Carbs: 30g | Protein: 18g | Fat: 5g

Creamy Mushroom Risotto

 2 servings 🕐 30 minutes

INGREDIENTS

- 1/2 cup Arborio rice
- 1 cup low-sodium chicken or vegetable broth
- 1/4 cup low-fat milk or lactose-free milk
- 1/2 cup finely chopped mushrooms
- Salt and pepper to taste
- 1 teaspoon olive oil

DIRECTIONS

1. In a saucepan, heat olive oil over medium heat. Add the chopped mushrooms and sauté until softened, about 3-4 minutes.
2. Stir in the Arborio rice and cook for an additional 1-2 minutes, stirring constantly.
3. Gradually add the broth, one ladle at a time, stirring frequently until the liquid is absorbed before adding more.
4. After about 15 minutes, when the rice is creamy and tender, stir in the milk and season with salt and pepper. Heat through before serving.

Nutritional Info per Serving: Calories: 210 | Carbs: 32g | Protein: 6g | Fat: 5g

Soft Zucchini and Cheese Bake

 2 servings   🕐 25 minutes

INGREDIENTS

- 1 medium zucchini, thinly sliced
- 1/2 cup low-fat cottage cheese
- 1/4 cup low-fat shredded mozzarella cheese
- 1 egg, beaten
- Salt and pepper to taste
- 1 teaspoon dried basil (optional)

DIRECTIONS

1. Preheat the oven to 375°F (190°C). In a mixing bowl, combine the zucchini slices, cottage cheese, mozzarella cheese, beaten egg, salt, pepper, and basil (if using).
2. Pour the mixture into a small baking dish and spread evenly.
3. Bake for 20-25 minutes, or until the top is set and golden.
4. Allow to cool slightly before serving.

Nutritional Info per Serving: Calories: 180 | Carbs: 10g | Protein: 15g | Fat: 7g

Snack Recipes

Smooth Banana Yogurt

 1 serving 5 minutes

INGREDIENTS

- 1 ripe banana
- 1/2 cup low-fat yogurt or lactose-free yogurt
- 1 teaspoon honey (optional, for sweetness)

DIRECTIONS

1. Peel the banana and place it in a bowl. Mash it until smooth.
2. Stir in the yogurt until well combined. If desired, add honey for sweetness.
3. Serve immediately or refrigerate for a refreshing snack.

Nutritional Info per Serving: Calories: 150 | Carbs: 30g | Protein: 6g | Fat: 1g

Rice Cake with Cottage Cheese

 1 serving   🕐 5 minutes

INGREDIENTS

- 1 plain rice cake
- 1/2 cup low-fat cottage cheese
- Pinch of salt and pepper (optional)

DIRECTIONS

1. Place the rice cake on a plate.
2. Spread the cottage cheese evenly over the rice cake.
3. Sprinkle with a pinch of salt and pepper if desired. Enjoy immediately!

Nutritional Info per Serving: Calories: 120 | Carbs: 14g | Protein: 11g | Fat: 2g

Applesauce with Cinnamon

 1 serving   5 minutes

INGREDIENTS

- 1/2 cup unsweetened applesauce
- 1/4 teaspoon ground cinnamon
- A few drops of lemon juice (optional)

DIRECTIONS

1. In a small bowl, combine the applesauce and ground cinnamon.
2. Add a few drops of lemon juice for extra flavor, if desired.
3. Stir well and serve chilled or at room temperature.

Nutritional Info per Serving: Calories: 50 | Carbs: 13g | Protein: 0g | Fat: 0g

Creamy Avocado Dip with Soft Tortilla

 1 serving   🕐 10 minutes

INGREDIENTS

- 1/2 ripe avocado
- 1 tablespoon low-fat Greek yogurt
- Pinch of salt
- 1 soft corn tortilla

DIRECTIONS

1. In a small bowl, mash the avocado until smooth.
2. Mix in the Greek yogurt and a pinch of salt until well combined.
3. Warm the corn tortilla slightly in a microwave or on a skillet until soft.
4. Spread the avocado dip on the tortilla, roll it up, and enjoy!

Nutritional Info per Serving: Calories: 180 | Carbs: 20g | Protein: 5g | Fat: 9g

Soft-Cooked Carrot Sticks

 1 serving   🕐 15 minutes

INGREDIENTS

- 1 medium carrot, peeled and cut into sticks
- 1 tablespoon low-fat ranch dressing or hummus (optional for dipping)

DIRECTIONS

1. In a small pot, bring water to a boil. Add the carrot sticks and cook for about 8-10 minutes, or until they are very tender.
2. Drain and allow to cool slightly.
3. Serve with low-fat ranch dressing or hummus for dipping, if desired.

Nutritional Info per Serving: Calories: 60 | Carbs: 14g | Protein: 1g | Fat: 0g

Creamy Potato and Cheese Bites

 2 servings   🕐 20 minutes

INGREDIENTS

- 1 medium potato, peeled and cubed
- 1/4 cup low-fat cheddar cheese, shredded
- Salt and pepper to taste

DIRECTIONS

1. Boil the cubed potato in salted water for about 10-12 minutes, or until tender.
2. Drain and mash the potato until smooth. Stir in the shredded cheese until melted and well combined.
3. Let cool slightly before shaping into small bite-sized balls or serving in a small bowl.

Nutritional Info per Serving: Calories: 130 | Carbs: 25g | Protein: 5g | Fat: 2g

Creamy Pumpkin Pudding

 1 serving   🕐 10 minutes

INGREDIENTS

- 1/2 cup canned pumpkin puree (not pumpkin pie filling)
- 1/4 cup low-fat milk or lactose-free milk
- 1 tablespoon honey or maple syrup (optional)
- 1/2 teaspoon ground cinnamon

DIRECTIONS

1. In a mixing bowl, combine the pumpkin puree, low-fat milk, honey or maple syrup (if using), and cinnamon.
2. Whisk until smooth and creamy.
3. Serve chilled or at room temperature.

Nutritional Info per Serving: Calories: 120 | Carbs: 27g | Protein: 4g | Fat: 1g

Soft Cheese and Melon Plate

 1 serving   🕐 5 minutes

INGREDIENTS

- 1/2 cup cantaloupe or honeydew melon, cubed
- 2 ounces low-fat cream cheese or ricotta cheese
- 1 teaspoon honey (optional)

DIRECTIONS

1. On a plate, arrange the melon cubes.
2. Serve with a side of low-fat cream cheese or ricotta cheese for dipping.
3. Drizzle with honey if desired.

Nutritional Info per Serving: Calories: 150 | Carbs: 18g | Protein: 6g | Fat: 6g

Sweet Potato Mash with Cinnamon

 1 serving 15 minutes

INGREDIENTS

- 1 small sweet potato, peeled and cubed
- 1 tablespoon low-fat milk or lactose-free milk
- 1/2 teaspoon ground cinnamon
- Pinch of salt

DIRECTIONS

1. Boil the cubed sweet potato in salted water for about 10-12 minutes or until tender.
2. Drain and return to the pot. Mash the sweet potato with a fork or potato masher.
3. Stir in the low-fat milk, cinnamon, and a pinch of salt until creamy and smooth. Serve warm.

Nutritional Info per Serving: Calories: 140 | Carbs: 30g | Protein: 2g | Fat: 0g

Creamy Avocado and Banana Mash

 1 serving   🕐 5 minutes

INGREDIENTS

- 1/2 ripe avocado
- 1/2 ripe banana
- 1 tablespoon low-fat yogurt (optional)

DIRECTIONS

1. In a small bowl, mash the avocado and banana together until smooth.
2. If desired, mix in the low-fat yogurt for extra creaminess.
3. Serve immediately as a dip or spread.

Nutritional Info per Serving: Calories: 180 | Carbs: 25g | Protein: 3g | Fat: 8g

Soft-Cooked Egg with Seasoned Mashed Potatoes

 1 serving   🕐 10 minutes

INGREDIENTS

- 1 large egg
- 1/2 cup mashed potatoes (made with low-fat milk)
- Pinch of salt and pepper (optional)

DIRECTIONS

1. Boil water in a small pot and gently add the egg. Cook for about 6-7 minutes for a soft-cooked egg.
2. Meanwhile, prepare the mashed potatoes with low-fat milk, adding a pinch of salt and pepper if desired.
3. Once the egg is cooked, peel and serve alongside the creamy mashed potatoes.

Nutritional Info per Serving: Calories: 210 | Carbs: 25g | Protein: 8g | Fat: 7g

Silken Tofu with Honey and Cinnamon

 1 serving   5 minutes

INGREDIENTS

- 1/2 cup silken tofu
- 1 tablespoon honey
- 1/4 teaspoon ground cinnamon

DIRECTIONS

1. In a small bowl, scoop the silken tofu.
2. Drizzle honey over the tofu and sprinkle with ground cinnamon.
3. Gently mix together and enjoy as a creamy, sweet snack.

Nutritional Info per Serving: Calories: 130 | Carbs: 25g | Protein: 5g | Fat: 3g

Baked Sweet Potato Chips

 1 serving   20 minutes

INGREDIENTS

- 1 small sweet potato, thinly sliced
- 1 teaspoon olive oil
- Pinch of salt

DIRECTIONS

1. Preheat the oven to 400°F (200°C). Line a baking sheet with parchment paper.
2. In a bowl, toss the sweet potato slices with olive oil and salt until evenly coated.
3. Arrange the slices in a single layer on the baking sheet.
4. Bake for 15-20 minutes, flipping halfway through, until the edges are crispy.
5. Allow to cool slightly before serving.

Nutritional Info per Serving: Calories: 120 | Carbs: 28g | Protein: 2g | Fat: 4g

Soft-Cooked Quinoa with Applesauce

 1 serving 🕐 15 minutes

INGREDIENTS

- 1/4 cup cooked quinoa
- 1/4 cup unsweetened applesauce
- 1/4 teaspoon ground cinnamon (optional)

DIRECTIONS

1. In a small saucepan, combine the cooked quinoa and applesauce. Heat gently over low heat until warm.
2. Stir in the ground cinnamon if desired.
3. Serve warm as a comforting snack.

Nutritional Info per Serving: Calories: 150 | Carbs: 30g | Protein: 5g | Fat: 1g

Yogurt and Soft Fruit Parfait

 1 serving   🕐 5 minutes

INGREDIENTS

- 1/2 cup low-fat yogurt (plain or flavored)
- 1/4 cup canned peaches or pears (in juice or water), drained and chopped
- 1 teaspoon honey (optional)

DIRECTIONS

1. In a small glass or bowl, layer the low-fat yogurt and chopped peaches or pears.
2. Drizzle honey on top if desired.
3. Enjoy immediately or chill for a refreshing treat.

Nutritional Info per Serving: Calories: 150 | Carbs: 24g | Protein: 7g | Fat: 3g

CONCLUSION

Living with both diabetes and gastroparesis is undeniably challenging, but with the right strategies and an informed approach, it is entirely possible to navigate these conditions with confidence and resilience.

Throughout this book, we've explored how these two conditions impact the body and why a tailored, mindful diet is crucial for managing symptoms and maintaining overall health.

A well-structured diet—focusing on low-fat, low-fiber, and easily digestible foods —plays an essential role in stabilizing blood sugar while reducing the digestive discomfort that gastroparesis brings.

The recipes and guidelines provided are designed to offer not only nourishment but also enjoyment, helping you reclaim a sense of control and joy around food.

This journey requires patience and adaptability. What works well one day might need adjusting the next, as both diabetes and gastroparesis can be unpredictable.

Listening to your body and observing how it responds to different foods and meal patterns is key.

Small, frequent meals are generally easier on digestion and prevent blood sugar fluctuations, and gentle cooking methods such as steaming, baking, and pureeing can make foods more tolerable.

For each meal, consider the nutrient balance while keeping portions manageable. This is a learning process, and it's perfectly normal to experiment with different foods and cooking techniques until you find what works best for you.

Beyond the physical aspects, managing diabetes and gastroparesis involves a holistic approach that includes mental and emotional well-being. Meal planning, symptom management, and blood sugar monitoring can feel overwhelming, so remember to be kind to yourself.

Seeking support from family, friends, and healthcare professionals can make a tremendous difference, offering encouragement, practical tips, and reassurance on days when things feel tough.

Additionally, staying informed and advocating for your needs is empowering; the more you know about how these conditions interact, the more effectively you can communicate with your care team to adjust treatments and dietary plans as needed.

While there are no one-size-fits-all solutions, adopting a positive, flexible approach to your dietary choices and lifestyle adjustments can make each day more manageable.

This book has equipped you with a toolkit of strategies, from understanding the science behind diabetes and gastroparesis to practical meal planning tips and recipes tailored for comfort and nutritional balance.

As you move forward, continue to explore what brings you comfort, stability, and satisfaction in your meals, knowing that each small step contributes to your well-being.

Managing these conditions is a journey, not a destination, and you are already equipped with the knowledge and resilience to handle whatever challenges may come your way.

RECIPE JOURNAL

RECIPE NAME : ....

....

....

NO. OF SERVINGS

TOTAL TIME

INGREDIENTS:

- ○ ....
- ○ ....
- ○ ....
- ○ ....
- ○ ....

- ○ ....
- ○ ....
- ○ ....
- ○ ....
- ○ ....

INSTRUCTIONS:

....

....

....

....

....

NOTES :

RECIPE JOURNAL

RECIPE NAME : ....
....
....

NO. OF SERVINGS

TOTAL TIME

INGREDIENTS:

- ○ ....
- ○ ....
- ○ ....
- ○ ....
- ○ ....

- ○ ....
- ○ ....
- ○ ....
- ○ ....
- ○ ....

INSTRUCTIONS:

....

....

....

....

....

NOTES :

RECIPE JOURNAL

RECIPE NAME :

....

....

....

NO. OF SERVINGS

TOTAL TIME

INGREDIENTS:

- ○ ....
- ○ ....
- ○ ....
- ○ ....
- ○ ....

- ○ ....
- ○ ....
- ○ ....
- ○ ....
- ○ ....

INSTRUCTIONS:

....

....

....

....

....

NOTES :

RECIPE JOURNAL

RECIPE NAME :

....

....

....

NO. OF SERVINGS

TOTAL TIME

INGREDIENTS:

- ○ ....
- ○ ....
- ○ ....
- ○ ....
- ○ ....

- ○ ....
- ○ ....
- ○ ....
- ○ ....
- ○ ....

INSTRUCTIONS:

....

....

....

....

....

NOTES :

RECIPE JOURNAL

RECIPE NAME :

....

....

....

NO. OF SERVINGS

TOTAL TIME

INGREDIENTS:

- ⚪ ....
- ⚪ ....
- ⚪ ....
- ⚪ ....
- ⚪ ....

- ⚪ ....
- ⚪ ....
- ⚪ ....
- ⚪ ....
- ⚪ ....

INSTRUCTIONS:

....

....

....

....

....

NOTES :

RECIPE JOURNAL

RECIPE NAME : ....

....

....

NO. OF SERVINGS

[...........................]

TOTAL TIME

[...........................]

INGREDIENTS:

○ ....   ○ ....

○ ....   ○ ....

○ ....   ○ ....

○ ....   ○ ....

○ ....   ○ ....

INSTRUCTIONS:

....

....

....

....

....

NOTES :

RECIPE JOURNAL

RECIPE NAME : ....

....

....

NO. OF SERVINGS

....

TOTAL TIME

....

INGREDIENTS:

- ○ ....
- ○ ....
- ○ ....
- ○ ....
- ○ ....

- ○ ....
- ○ ....
- ○ ....
- ○ ....
- ○ ....

INSTRUCTIONS:

....

....

....

....

....

NOTES :

RECIPE JOURNAL

RECIPE NAME :

....

....

....

NO. OF SERVINGS

TOTAL TIME

INGREDIENTS:

- ○ ....
- ○ ....
- ○ ....
- ○ ....
- ○ ....

- ○ ....
- ○ ....
- ○ ....
- ○ ....
- ○ ....

INSTRUCTIONS:

....

....

....

....

....

NOTES :

RECIPE JOURNAL

RECIPE NAME : ....
....
....

NO. OF SERVINGS

....

TOTAL TIME

....

INGREDIENTS:

○ ....   ○ ....
○ ....   ○ ....
○ ....   ○ ....
○ ....   ○ ....
○ ....   ○ ....

INSTRUCTIONS:

....
....
....
....
....

NOTES :

RECIPE JOURNAL

RECIPE NAME : ....

....

....

NO. OF SERVINGS

TOTAL TIME

INGREDIENTS:

- ○ ....
- ○ ....
- ○ ....
- ○ ....
- ○ ....

- ○ ....
- ○ ....
- ○ ....
- ○ ....
- ○ ....

INSTRUCTIONS:

....

....

....

....

....

NOTES :

RECIPE JOURNAL

RECIPE NAME : ....

....

....

NO. OF SERVINGS

....

TOTAL TIME

....

INGREDIENTS:

○ ....   ○ ....

○ ....   ○ ....

○ ....   ○ ....

○ ....   ○ ....

○ ....   ○ ....

INSTRUCTIONS:

....

....

....

....

....

NOTES :

RECIPE JOURNAL

RECIPE NAME :

....

....

....

NO. OF SERVINGS

TOTAL TIME

INGREDIENTS:

- ○ ....
- ○ ....
- ○ ....
- ○ ....
- ○ ....

- ○ ....
- ○ ....
- ○ ....
- ○ ....
- ○ ....

INSTRUCTIONS:

....

....

....

....

NOTES :

RECIPE JOURNAL

RECIPE NAME : ....
....
....

NO. OF SERVINGS

TOTAL TIME

INGREDIENTS:

- ○ ....
- ○ ....
- ○ ....
- ○ ....
- ○ ....

- ○ ....
- ○ ....
- ○ ....
- ○ ....
- ○ ....

INSTRUCTIONS:

....

....

....

....

NOTES :

RECIPE JOURNAL

RECIPE NAME : ....

....

....

NO. OF SERVINGS

TOTAL TIME

INGREDIENTS:

- ○ ....
- ○ ....
- ○ ....
- ○ ....
- ○ ....

- ○ ....
- ○ ....
- ○ ....
- ○ ....
- ○ ....

INSTRUCTIONS:

....

....

....

....

....

NOTES :

RECIPE JOURNAL

RECIPE NAME : ....
....
....

NO. OF SERVINGS

TOTAL TIME

INGREDIENTS:

- ○ ....
- ○ ....
- ○ ....
- ○ ....
- ○ ....

- ○ ....
- ○ ....
- ○ ....
- ○ ....
- ○ ....

INSTRUCTIONS:

....

....

....

....

....

NOTES :

RECIPE JOURNAL

RECIPE NAME :

....

....

NO. OF SERVINGS

....

TOTAL TIME

....

INGREDIENTS:

- ○ ....
- ○ ....
- ○ ....
- ○ ....
- ○ ....

- ○ ....
- ○ ....
- ○ ....
- ○ ....
- ○ ....

INSTRUCTIONS:

....

....

....

....

....

NOTES :

RECIPE JOURNAL

RECIPE NAME :
....
....
....

NO. OF SERVINGS

TOTAL TIME

INGREDIENTS:

- ○ ....
- ○ ....
- ○ ....
- ○ ....
- ○ ....

- ○ ....
- ○ ....
- ○ ....
- ○ ....
- ○ ....

INSTRUCTIONS:

....

....

....

....

....

NOTES :

RECIPE JOURNAL

RECIPE NAME : ....
....
....

NO. OF SERVINGS

TOTAL TIME

INGREDIENTS:

- ○ ....
- ○ ....
- ○ ....
- ○ ....
- ○ ....

- ○ ....
- ○ ....
- ○ ....
- ○ ....
- ○ ....

INSTRUCTIONS:

....

....

....

....

....

NOTES :

RECIPE JOURNAL

RECIPE NAME : ....

....

....

NO. OF SERVINGS

....

TOTAL TIME

....

INGREDIENTS:

- ○ ....
- ○ ....
- ○ ....
- ○ ....
- ○ ....

- ○ ....
- ○ ....
- ○ ....
- ○ ....
- ○ ....

INSTRUCTIONS:

....

....

....

....

....

NOTES :

RECIPE JOURNAL

RECIPE NAME :
....
....
....

NO. OF SERVINGS

TOTAL TIME

INGREDIENTS:

○ ....
○ ....
○ ....
○ ....
○ ....

○ ....
○ ....
○ ....
○ ....
○ ....

INSTRUCTIONS:

....
....
....
....
....

NOTES :

RECIPE JOURNAL

RECIPE NAME :

....

....

....

NO. OF SERVINGS

TOTAL TIME

INGREDIENTS:

- ○ ....
- ○ ....
- ○ ....
- ○ ....
- ○ ....

- ○ ....
- ○ ....
- ○ ....
- ○ ....
- ○ ....

INSTRUCTIONS:

....

....

....

....

....

NOTES :

RECIPE JOURNAL

RECIPE NAME :

....

....

....

NO. OF SERVINGS

TOTAL TIME

INGREDIENTS:

- ○ ....
- ○ ....
- ○ ....
- ○ ....
- ○ ....

- ○ ....
- ○ ....
- ○ ....
- ○ ....
- ○ ....

INSTRUCTIONS:

....

....

....

....

....

NOTES :

RECIPE JOURNAL

RECIPE NAME :

NO. OF SERVINGS

TOTAL TIME

INGREDIENTS:

- ○
- ○
- ○
- ○
- ○

- ○
- ○
- ○
- ○
- ○

INSTRUCTIONS:

NOTES :

RECIPE JOURNAL

RECIPE NAME : ....
....
....

NO. OF SERVINGS

[....]

TOTAL TIME

[....]

INGREDIENTS:

- ○ ....
- ○ ....
- ○ ....
- ○ ....
- ○ ....

- ○ ....
- ○ ....
- ○ ....
- ○ ....
- ○ ....

INSTRUCTIONS:

....

....

....

....

....

NOTES :

RECIPE JOURNAL

RECIPE NAME :

....

....

....

NO. OF SERVINGS

TOTAL TIME

INGREDIENTS:

- ○ ....
- ○ ....
- ○ ....
- ○ ....
- ○ ....

- ○ ....
- ○ ....
- ○ ....
- ○ ....
- ○ ....

INSTRUCTIONS:

....

....

....

....

....

NOTES :

RECIPE JOURNAL

RECIPE NAME : ....

....

....

NO. OF SERVINGS

TOTAL TIME

INGREDIENTS:

- ○ ....
- ○ ....
- ○ ....
- ○ ....
- ○ ....

- ○ ....
- ○ ....
- ○ ....
- ○ ....
- ○ ....

INSTRUCTIONS:

....

....

....

....

....

NOTES :

RECIPE JOURNAL

RECIPE NAME : ....

....

....

NO. OF SERVINGS

....

TOTAL TIME

....

INGREDIENTS:

○ ....

○ ....

○ ....

○ ....

○ ....

○ ....

○ ....

○ ....

○ ....

○ ....

INSTRUCTIONS:

....

....

....

....

....

NOTES :

RECIPE JOURNAL

RECIPE NAME : ....

....

....

NO. OF SERVINGS

[..................................]

TOTAL TIME

[..................................]

INGREDIENTS:

- ○ ....
- ○ ....
- ○ ....
- ○ ....
- ○ ....

- ○ ....
- ○ ....
- ○ ....
- ○ ....
- ○ ....

INSTRUCTIONS:

....

....

....

....

....

NOTES :

RECIPE JOURNAL

RECIPE NAME :

....

....

....

NO. OF SERVINGS

TOTAL TIME

INGREDIENTS:

- ⃝ ....
- ⃝ ....
- ⃝ ....
- ⃝ ....
- ⃝ ....

- ⃝ ....
- ⃝ ....
- ⃝ ....
- ⃝ ....
- ⃝ ....

INSTRUCTIONS:

....

....

....

....

....

NOTES :

RECIPE JOURNAL

RECIPE NAME :

....

....

....

NO. OF SERVINGS

[   ]

TOTAL TIME

[   ]

INGREDIENTS:

- ○ ....
- ○ ....
- ○ ....
- ○ ....
- ○ ....

- ○ ....
- ○ ....
- ○ ....
- ○ ....
- ○ ....

INSTRUCTIONS:

....

....

....

....

....

NOTES :

Made in the USA
Columbia, SC
30 April 2025

57354449R00061